THE RUBICON

BY RAS HERU

ISBN: 978-1-7324557-6-4

LCCN: 2020948989

Cover Design by Dayana Poulard & Ras Heru

Photography by Matt Pierce and Ameerah Shabazz-Bilal

Book Design and Publishing by Rebel Ink Publishing

First printing edition 2020

Foreword

by Ameerah Shabazz-Bilal

To take a course of no return... To make a commitment that forces an irreversible action… Like, time spinning... Impossible. You are now, and forever will be, right here in this moment. What are you going to do about it?

With *The Rubicon*, Ras Heru has spun a course for readers that propels us down an often-rugged and always-turbulent journey which, of course, you cannot deviate from once you have begun. You cannot go back. You will be changed, willingly or unwillingly, for his words will not release you until their objectives are met.

What is the consequence? Walking with kings, traversing narrow paths of love, and laying sight to un-shoveled fears and thoughts of how you may have been, will be, or are currently being, conquered. Surrender. *The Rubicon* will make all known to you; the author is truthful in this promise.

Ras is masterful in his analogies of love, life, broken spirits and hearts as he throws his own decisive moments out for you to cross over. Whether it be in the full armor of a Roman warrior or a Black American trumpeter of lost and found loves and hurts, or Ras crafting war cries against injustice on the behalf of the masses…beware, these captivating stories await and, indeed, they will change you. Forever.

Contents

Populares pg. 80

A Soothsayer's Promise

In Celebration of a Fatal Baptism

Proscriptions 1: A Love Letter to Black Bodies

Proscriptions 2: An Incomplete List

This Poem is Important

Succession (Nipsey's Poem)

Letters: to The Legions (Can't Stop, Won't Stop)

Commentaries pg. 135

Wings

Letters: to The Senate

Letters: to Brutus

Letters: to the Daggers

The Rubicon/Epilogue: A Final Decree pg. 158

IMPERIUM

The word *imperium,* commonly used synonymously with words like *power* or *authority,* under Roman law meant *authority to command.* During the Late Republic of Rome (roughly 133 BCE - 31 BCE) leading commanders of the Roman state with *imperium* had the legal authority to raise and command military forces (Rome at the time did not have a singular, State-sponsored military) and to use those forces as they saw fit, typically against foreign threat or for Roman conquest, with the formal approval and guidelines agreed to by the Roman Senate.

At the end of Gaius Julius Caesar's governorship and expansion of Roman rule over Gallic lands – a roughly 8 to 9 year span during which he doubled the size of his army as well as the amount of territory that now belonged to Rome (or, arguably, to Caesar) - he and his army were headed back to Rome. Caesar was intending to qualify himself for a second consulship – the highest political office of Rome – and in doing so, introduce reform policies to alleviate land inequalities, refine prior policies that had taken advantage of Rome's poorer classes for generations, and also compensate his veterans for their years of service to his conquests (which at times were not sanctioned or supported by the Roman Senate).

Recognizing Caesar's intent and probable success at securing a second consulship, the Senate - led by many of Caesar's personal, political enemies - issued a decree that Caesar lie down his *imperium,* abandon his army at the border, and enter Rome as a formal/private citizen, to be prosecuted on charges of illegal and unsanctioned activity in Gaul (curiously, the Senate shared in the spoils sent by Caesar from Gaul throughout these years).

Famously ignoring this mandate, Caesar took a small portion of his army and forwarded toward the northern Roman border, outlined by the Rubicon River. Crossing this small, shallow river assured that Rome would soon see civil war as the act of any commander – Roman or not – entering Rome with an active military backing of any size was viewed as an active declaration of war. Legend has it, Caesar announced *"the die is cast!"* essentially meaning *"the dice has been rolled, and there is no turning back!"* just as he and a portion of his army forwarded into Rome. Crossing the Rubicon was a turning point not just in the lives of Julius Caesar, his opponents, his and their soldiers, and all the rest of Rome, but also a turning point in what would become today known as Western Civilization. Nowadays, the terms *crossing the rubicon* and *having a rubicon moment* have become metaphors for *taking an irrevocable course of action* — an action that cannot be reset or abandoned once made, and that permanently changes the future from what otherwise could have been.

Outbreak/The Crossing

THIS is the start of civil war.

THIS is a commentary

on the carnage unravelling

within since *Mother was split* [1] on the 13th

of a Friday in Fall,

THIS

is the Hall of Records in which you will find

the catalogues of marches I've led, at times

against my own right mind,

meaning THIS

this is a chronicle of an olive branch alchemized

into a noose, the tragic tale

of a dove frantically gasping for air:

the future declared dead,

my inequities suited, booted, and spread

in homicidal formations awaiting the trumpets to sound the

beginning of the slaughter, meaning THIS

is the genesis of the genocide and *I? I?*

Well…

      I am a **bad joke…**

waiting to be rewritten, I am…

fruit forbidden from all the tongues of ones wishing

to remain safe, I am

the escape room **with really no**

escape at all…

I am!

I am Julius Caesar's *Achilles' Heel* [2], I am

when keeping it real ain't right,

I mean

when keeping it real is really, really *wrong*

I mean

I am the song your grandma told you only "fast kids" dance

to…

I am the sweet that will leave you sour. I will devour

All of the flowers in your garden as pretty things with

potential and possibility at life seem to be the only things that

satiate my appetite

and *I promise...*

I promise to ruin you if you let me.
I promise to be the worst thing you've ever loved,

I promise to be the pool of tears of
which you thought you were prepared to wade,

the charade of escapades you thought you could persuade
into some sort of sanity -

I promise! I promise

to be everything you never wanted, wrapped in everything

that has ever delivered you satisfaction,

I promise, I promise

to be your doom,

I promise

to consume you…

the moment you place me at your lips and light me; I promise

to lift you,

I promise to **leave you**

high…

helpless, and handled, (unless you are ready to discard with

me now)

I promise

to ruin you.

poem notes

---

1 – The term *C-Section* is short for *Caesarean Section,* which Caesar's mother actually did not have (though Ras Heru's mother did).

2 – someone's *Achilles's Heel,* metaphorically, is their fatal weakness, or the cause of their downfall

A Cautionary Tale about Stones

I am the stone that should forever be refused.

I am the fiasco fabricated -

attempting to take shape behind the facade

of pretty poems, I

am the pretty that is poison. I

am the cautionary tale told about poets, I

am the shine that will blind you, please

take caution. Take care

as all I have to spare you is

the allure of things,

the charm of the *Sirens* [1],

a price tag that you will ultimately wish

you could not afford,

a perfume that will never amount to more

than the stench of bad memories, I am

the *MOURNING*…

after the party.

Something like what is left behind
from destructive combinations of ill intentions and wrong
decisions, I am

ambition unhinged.

I am the binge that does not sleep,
I am a crude apology forever unable to weep,

I am a coming storm, sick

of its own forecast, a lasting
trauma with a talent for leaving impressions
on the life you used to know…

    I wasn't asked for
        and I know it.

Great republics have fallen because of me.
Families have been introduced to carnage
because of my sword's thirst for glory,

a story told for thousands of years that still ends

in the same bloody mess,

blessed and obsessed with *the power to rearrange*

your calendar [4], I can assure you your days are numbered

should you choose not to heed my warning,

I'M WORN OUT!

MY EYES HAVE SWALLOWED MORE THAN BONES
CAN CARRY. MY LIVER CAN TELL YOU STORIES
THAT MY LEADERS WOULD SHAME. MY NAME
HAS BEEN MANY THINGS ACROSS THE YEARS
THOUGH IT HAS NEVER REALLY MATTERED,

they say,

all is fair

in love and war…

But what they always fail to tell you

is that semantics is really all that separates the two.

What they always fail to tell you

is that there is no matter between mortals that can't be

summarized as an act of one or an act of the other.

What they always fail to tell you

is all that decides which is which is where you are standing

when the sword is unsheathed.

What they always fail to tell you

is that what you love will break you.

What they always fail to tell you is there are no winners

in war, all that's left from the siege are the dead and the

traumatized,

THE DEAD AND THE TRAUMATIZED,

THE DEAD AND THE TRAUMATIZED,

THE DEAD AND THE TRAUMATIZED!

I TELL YOU! I AM THE STONE!

Ask *Goliath* [2] about my damage…
Ask *Debo* [3] what a brick can do…

ask them both how dirt tastes,

ask them both if the sleep is any more peaceful
after the fall,

ask yourself if you are really, really ready to cast the die
and risk it all

       on a stone already warning you …

to never entrust it with your dreams,
never build your sand castles upon me

because when the battle lines have been broken,
and sunrise has come to greet the Earth at dawn,

all that will be left

are

THE DEAD AND THE TRAUMATIZED.

THE DEAD AND THE TRAUMATIZED,

THE DEAD AND THE TRAUMATIZED,

THE DEAD AND THE TRAUMATIZED.

poem notes

———————————————————————————————

1 – in Greek mythology, *sirens* were beautiful and tempting sea creatures that would lure sailors into fatally crashing their ships

2 – the giant, biblical character defeated by young David's rock to the forehead

3 – the antagonist and bully of the cult-classic film *Friday*

4 -the Julian Calendar, established by Caesar after returning from winning the Civil War and seeing how the city and Senate had been manipulating the calendar and exploiting the discord as a result. This calendar is scarcely different from, and is, the main source for the *Gregorian Calendar,* that most the world uses today.

A Poem about Things I'm Not Sure of

I have a confession to make:

I'm not quite so gentle all of the time. Most of the time though, I'm okay with this.

You see…My mother's first name is *Patricia* [1]. Her last name is a city in Italy,

and though she has never been,
I was raised by Black women with colosseums
in their bones,

sometimes, sometimes

I write poems from places where pressure and persuasion go to dance beneath the moon.

I admit I am never ever quite able to get a firm footing over the rhythm of the music, though on the other hand, my pen?

My pen seems to be capable of handling panic quite well, and frankly sometimes…sometimes it makes me jealous.

Sometimes…

I try and sleep and I can hear the ghastly gallop of a gladiator's horse. I lie awake wondering if the stampedes I feel in my chest can reveal just why I know so much about the fall of empires,

I toss and turn hoping my pen can be as lethal as a Roman soldier's sword and then I concern myself with why…

why I choose to compare something that gives me life to an instrument designed to draw blood, I question

what is it about blood
that makes me pour into these lines…

What is it about glory that makes us seek out our destruction?

What is it about the soil
that makes us feed it dead bodies?

poem notes

---

1 – the *patricians* were the upper class society of Rome

The Streets of Home (Or, A Poem About Newark)

Let the headlines tell it…

there is never a wrong day for somebody, somewhere,
to catch a body where I'm from.

In defense of the Truth,
you let me tell it and I will tell you

such a statement isn't really all that inaccurate.

A punchline packed with enough potent truth
to crack your funny bone; I can promise you
the streets of Home are no joking matter.

Name the smoke you want,
I know a block that will bring it.

Streets are always watching, yet
nobody ever seen it.

A city well acclaimed

for both its infamy and fame, you know

the name

I dare you say it!

Pronunciation of the word is the test

of your survival [1]*, known*

to champion your cause or for picking off

your brightest idol;

what's in the water? What's in the water?

X marks the spot

of the ballroom plot,

what's in the water? What's in the water! [2]

City Man, what's the plan! What you keepin' in the closet?

Corrosion of the soul, now the weapon is the faucet!

What's the cost of current losses?

A city's worth of blues, but what else is city news?

Camera crews point and shoot like how a gangster makes his

bones, a taker's *itch for Good Times* [3] will have your *Happy*

Days [4] postponed,

where I'm from…where I'm from

is no television sitcom. Hunger pains and quests for change

will make a man do anything but sit calm,

the wrong line crossed can have your jaw rearranged,

a natural attraction to flames, we

are always just around the corner from a riot *(or rebellion?* [4]*)*,

always just up the block from disseminating our latest set

of ass whoopings,

only 5 minutes away, always, from catching

the next come-up, only ever needing half a reason to activate

a run up … I love it here!

Contribute a *New Ark* [5] to your novel,

solidify with brute force what a pen can't make clean,
pivotal yet far from pristine,

the rawest and realest glimpse of a world
you've never seen.

Black hoodies and *Miskeens* [6], bean pies and *Final Calls* [7],
brothers and sisters out to get it
will turn your corner block into a strip mall,
I tell you the streets of Home are like the streets of Rome.

And as a *Native Son* [8],
I am here to assure you that the *Bigger* [9] I get,

the more you should be concerned with me.
For what reason? Pick one for I'm sure they're all valid.

Brilliant, beautiful, barbarous and otherwise not always safe,
even lethal on the wrong day, my point is…

the headlines are only slightly off-base,
politicized against me sure, but not always wrong…

Name your valor, name your vice, villainy or virtue, I assure you, it all leads to here. Starts here. Stops here.

The streets of Home.

poem notes

---

1 – Newarkers can spot outsiders by how they fully pronounce the city's name, whereas most Newarker's naturally say "Nork"

2 – references to the Water Crisis in Newark/Essex county, as well as the widely-regarded belief that the chief assassins in the murder of Malcolm X held from Newark, NJ

3 – names of two popular American sitcoms

4 – reference to the Newark Riot/Rebellion of 1967

5 – *New Ark* was the original/intended name of the city at its settling

6 – a popular clothing brand in the early 2000s that was prevalently worn in Newark

7 – the official newspaper of the National of Islam

8 – the title of the famous American novel by Richard Wright

9 – the protagonist of *Native Son*

Imperium

I heard the word could raise an army.
I heard that all the idioms and juxtapositions
between pens and swords were bullshit.

I once watched in awe
while a poet rose a *legion* [1] in my veins
with a poem that you could swear
knew everything

there was to know about deadly edges
and cold truths

and yet
with every slash and lunge
of her weapon she stitched me
into a soldier,

my blood the temperature of belief,
her cadence proof

that generals and griots carried

the same fully loaded clips,

and since then I've been convinced…

that between my lips I hold the power
to make or break Earth,

that with the mite of my own will I could do wild shit like:

order a hurricane to stand still,

could make a corpse of a caring heart,
can make soldiers of mortal souls,
can make martyrs of those dying
for something to believe in,

I suggest…

I suggest
you incorporate terms like *arsenal, warfare,* and *never surrender*
from now on when you speak to me of poems,

fighting

is the only formation most of my stanzas have ever known,

listen close

to the meter and in every line you can hear a different city

under siege,

I mean

so much civil war, suicide, and strife

within these binds that rumor has it you can find

my next collection of poems in the obituaries.

Scary, the thought.

Horrifying, the reality.

Pen, sword, bullet, or tongue, either the case…

the blood is still red.

The casket and the dirt are both cold,

and the thirst for bone and glory

is still all that will, forever, remain eternal.

poem notes

---

1 – the main units of the Roman army at the time, containing 4000 – 5000 soldiers

Snap

"I am inevitable", said the Monster.

I am the future you cannot escape. Look at me!
See me draped in dazzling metals and precious stones,
look at me!

Gaze upon this throne I intend to sit upon the heap of ashes
that was once a world you loved,

I said

LOOK AT ME!

Your *powers* [1] of persuasion will fail you here!

No matters of *space* [1] or *time* [1] will mend the *reality* [1]
that Fate has got its *mind* [1] made up, I

have got my mind made up. You

may acknowledge me by whatever name might;
fear me not as, sooner or later, the night finally catches us all!

The only question that remains is…

who mourns the *souls* [1] that don't survive the middle passage?

What comfort can be provided to those among you
unworthy of even the dust that proceeds the snap?

poem notes

---

1 – the names of the 6 infinity stones of the Marvel Universe

---

SCORCHED

EARTH

As pivotal as crossing the Rubicon was to the legacies of Caesar, Rome, and the Western world, so were the years and battles waged across the vast Gallic lands leading up to the crossing, where victory after victory gave Caesar the fortitude to believe both in his prowess for winning war but also his talent and knack for facilitating peace. The underbelly of that empowering fortitude to take on the world though are the piles of countless bodies, the many rivers turned red, and the history of virtually all Gallic culture and existence reduced to rubble - their lands penetrated with Roman banners, their lives now lived in the service of the ancient, imperial superpower that was Rome.

Scorched Earth refers to a defensive battle tactic used against Caesar's legions by their fiercest Gallic enemies, but it also metaphorically connotes all the bones and tragedies upon which all our favorite heroic stories are built. How many people have had to meet tragic fates in one man's route for glory? How many lives have been forced to change because they had no choice but to bend to a conqueror's desires? How many homes have you broken? How many homes haven't healed? What becomes of a man who has shed so much blood?

Scorched Earth

Cover the ground

in chaos.

Send word to the soil

that the fire wants its day.

Give notice to the flowers

of the tax now that lie upon

their petals and

and save prayer

for those among us too stubborn

to perish

after the scorch because

I don't remember the last thing I loved

that I didn't set

on fire.

In the fight to defend against the Romans,

Gallic leader Vercingetorix

ordered the burning

of all home lands,

towns, and territories

in so

to deprive the enemy

of the possibility to plunder and

I wonder...

if my predilection for feeding

the appetites of flames with the things I value most

is how I defend against the ghosts

that history has already assigned

to destroy me.

I wonder if my hands are always warm

because I am perpetually liable to combust.

I wonder if the smell of gasoline is the reason why

I wrote my first poem.

I am sure, by now, that I have become

a thermometer's worst nightmare.

I am sure, by now, that me and the Sun

have developed a territorial beef. Just as well

that by now, I am sure

that loving me is the closest to Hell

you will ever come

without having to first kiss

the reaper.

A Poem on Ego and Decadence

My campaign is champagne sponsored;

I've conquered everywhere that you care to know about;

my clout is cosmic with those familiar with the forest

beyond the frontline weeds, I bleed a purple that is beyond

your conception of noble truth;

Noble Drew [1] taught me to talk like this. *Nina Simone* [2] wrote

the poems that made me invincible, and so it is only sensible

that your knees make acquaintance with the ground when you

hear the sound of my voice: I am the choice you have been

given. I am the offer you cannot refuse, the muse for your

tomorrow, the coming of your sorrow, frankly

Caesar would sure as hell had bet the bank on me had he not

met *Octavian* [3] first,

I am the Year 3000! …

TRAPPED

in 29 years that came a millennium before it,

I learned to shoot dice from drug dealers; my Mother taught me *Supreme Mathematics* [4], I say all of this to say there has never been a realer specimen as I. Cut

from diamonds, which may explain why I am decadent by design; comparable to only *Pablo* [5] in his prime,

pick your preference, though most of my kind would agree that there is but little difference between art and drugs anyway [5],

anyway…

If you think there isn't a landmass large enough to land my ego, you are correct. Make no mistake,

I think of me exactly what you think I think of me

and it is not entirely my fault. The sages spoke it so. History shows that my lineage has been known for producing lions long before me. I am highly, I mean *Haile* [6] accustomed to kingship and, at this point, you expect it from me,

I require no thank-you's for my service.

The favor upon which I call continuously unto you is simple:
be your own damn Hero.

Take slight from no one and make ghosts of those who fail to
hail the god in you.

Be not convinced that you are not *Zeus* [7] incarnate unless you
have sunken low enough to believe it not so,

and if indeed you have arrived as such feeble conclusions…

start this poem from the top. Put *Reasonable Doubt* [8] on vinyl.
Watch the movie Malcolm X. Read a Toni Morrison novel.
Imagine

yourself painting the *Mona Lisa* [9]…inhale a bit deeper…

and knock it the fuck off.

poem notes

1 – Nobel Drew Ali was a spiritual leader who established the Moorish Science Temple in Newark, NJ, 1913. Their beliefs in regards to Black Spirituality and social/religious progression for Black people were a predecessor and inspiration for other social and religious Black nationalist groups that followed.

2 – Nina Simone is an iconic, legendary musician and Black Liberationist

3 – Octavian, the young, politically-astute great-nephew of Caesar and his chosen heir, who would be the last participant standing in the decade of civil war sparked by Caesar's death. He would become "Augustus Caesar", the first official emperor of Rome, who went on to bring peace and stability to Rome during his reign, which would last roughly 40 years.

4 – Supreme Mathematics is a numeral system that relates numbers to higher, philosophical understandings that empower those that study and apply the system, created and practiced by the Nation of Gods & Earths (otherwise known as 5 Percenters).

5 – Pablo Picasso/Pablo Escobar

6 - Haile Selassie is the 225th (and last) Emperor of Ethiopia. Known as Ras Tafari before his coronation, his 40 year reign beginning in 1930 provided a contribution to Ethiopia, Africa, and the world in a way inspired Black people of the west to gather under what would become the Rastafari Movement, of which Haile Selassie is recognized as the highest and most central figure

7 – Zeus is the god of the sky, lightning and the thunder Greek Mythology

8 – The debut album of Jay Z

9 – The famous painting by Leonardo Di Vinci

Have You Ever Seen the Reign?

I am the unconquered.

When provoked, or otherwise bothered

I invoke the spirits

that make men immortal

and cowards kings,

so in the face of tyranny I sing

songs of strength, tell me please

have you ever seen the reign?

A wrecking ball's kiss

to any obstacle out to stop me,

I consider a *gauntlet thrown* [1] to be an act of romance

and I'll dance with whomever.

I ask you again

  have you ever

seen the reign?

I know every single genre of seduction, plus

    I know why warfare is sexy,

I am here for the feast and not

selfish in the least,

no surrender and no retreats,

the legions

would love a leader like me.

Decreed in more than just the art of war

I can assure you a new era:

a policy that provides,

a dominion over the darkness that resides

both inside and out,

an empire that never sees the Sun set,

a living example of the phrase

if I ain't dead, then I ain't done yet,

a soldier's silhouette and a polymath's mind,

a kind man and a jealous god, I gave New York insomnia way

back...*reduced Pompeii to ash the last time a city made me angry*

[2]...almost lost the Pyramids in a dice game!

I ask you again

have you ever seen a reign

like mine?

Call me commander, *Imperator* [3!]

set the stage so that my *triumph* [4] is grand;

may the people stand and band in the streets

for the feats accomplished in their name, no

I do not claim to be king as I am something far more

complex... I do not aim to be a god as I am something far

more original...

my status, seminal;

my principle is pivotal, my pinnacle achievement will be that

human history never forgets what we did here, so cheer me as

I cheer for you.

Let every corner of the globe hear us laugh. Dance hard enough to scare off anyone with weak hips.

Let them know that we live life fiercely, that we greet doubt with indignation, that Fate is but a loud mouth taking advantage of the fact that we both forgot who really is in charge here,

paint my face red, color my robe purple [5],
look to the future through whatever kaleidoscope you choose but do not doubt that the light we show the world today will change it tomorrow, make no mistake

I am no rainbow myself…Reach the pot of gold at the end of me and you will be just as likely to find dynamite, the real question is

just how high do you really, really want to be? Whatever your answer, believe

I got the gas for your trip…a résumé that stretches from here to the moon…the mite to make wrong right and right righter…

THIS is the part of the poem that summons your lighters to a
position above your shoulders, THIS is the part of the poem
where you decide to hold the spark in you so high that the
Sun has no choice but to file a grievance,

I guarantee,
you will never know a reign like mine;

and I'll finely dine in Hell, or be halfway to *Hades* [6]
before I sell myself short,
only resorting to wrath for tactical reason
and come this season,

you will know just why

my reign is
inevitable.

poem notes

---

1 – "throwing down the gauntlet" is a phrase that means issuing a challenge or an invitation for combat

2 – Pompeii – the historic Italian city that was destroyed by the eruption of Mount Vesuvius

3 – Imperator meant "commander" on the battlefield; this title remained with Caesar after the Civil War; "emperor" is derived from this word.

4 – A triumph, much like a parade today, was a public ceremony of celebration and feast, honoring a victorious returning general from war. These mass displays often also involved public feasts, gladiator games, and the parading of prisoners of war captured by the returning army

5 – activities associated with being a divine ruler and/or Royalty (which Roman citizens of the Late Republic hated and Caesar never claimed to be, though he would frequently engage in such dress while at the height of his power/just before his assassination)

6 – Greek god and king of the dead/underworld

Down the Nile

Regal, robust, replica of *Isis* [1],

sultry and cerebral sovereign presenting me
with crisis,

armed with trinkets,
charm, and an offer I can't refuse, Cleopatra Queen
I choose you.

Mind to the brim with ambition,
riotous curves keeping me away from *Home*
and out of commission [2],

I tell my intuitions no.

Naval Commander you are, across the waters we go.

Vacationing along this floating fantasy set to carry us
down the Nile, Cleopatra,

I confess

I've contemplated for quite a while your place at my side,
our futures fated and doomed to collide, Cleopatra besides…

I've taken notice to the superior strut in your stride
since the day I arrived,

  look at you...

Your eyes betray you. Your smile a most traitorous beauty,
without the words, you tell me

just how your highest temples have yearned for an
occupation of a Higher order,

how your borders are barren with broken wants,
how your fortress is but a front, Cleopatra,

how you wanted me to hunt you and I did,
you wanted me to want you and I did,

how you needed me to save you and I did,
how I wanted you to need me and you did,

so tell me how and why is it

cannot you get rid

of her.

My *imprint in need of empire* [3],

our collective fires set to turn our loins

into lions, it is lovers' alchemy

how we ravage each other and produce

a more potent self post-climax,

no kayak boats, ocean liner floats, or naval submarine

can intervene in the waterworld destruction

caused by our eruptions, Cleopatra

listen to you...

A newfound love for kingdom in your voice since the day

your tongue made acquaintance with the taste of my

imperium,

the fleeting thought of never returning to Rome

firmly besieging my better senses,

I declared you my favorite waterfall,
you christened me the *Son of Poseidon* [4],

not even Noah would know what to do
with a flood like ours, Cleopatra

send the word across the seas that the the world is ours,
Cleopatra, I command you not to cower
when the waves come crashing.

I summon you to keep solid when soldiers are at our gates,
I *demande* [5] you hold straight despite the crooked ways that
got us here,

Cleopatra,

I hope you hear me in the midst of this floating façade -
this honey moon ride before the doom,

I hope you know I mean business…

Years of battle keep my standards raised, plus
you know you've never known a rage like me,

never a purple more pure, never a force more sure
to turn your home into an urn,
Cleopatra, earn your keep
and concern yourself only of Us.

More than a wind's gust of a grand time,
I play for keeps. Sympathies

for all those who will weep, those who hate will have to hang
…on, I'm on you…

Cleopatra, like the mask you wear to masquerade what has
been manifested, I'm on you…

like sweat and nighttime skies painted across the back seat of
your ride, I'm on you…

Cleopatra, like ash on ankles, I'm on you…

like a damsel at my door at the end of a hard day,

Cleopatra, can you tell me truthfully that it will all be okay?

That I may love you as I wish.
That I may build my rock upon you.
That we may seal eternity with a kiss,

along the Nile, Cleopatra Queen, listen and know
denial shall never satisfy you,

just as the word "no" has never accomplished anything other
than inspire me to wreck homes and burn cities, Cleopatra…

I pity the alternative. Just as well as I warn you
that your fear of the waters

will be the reason
that we drown.

poem notes

---

1 – the Egyptian Goddess of whom Cleopatra claimed to be incarnate and whom after she fashioned herself.

2 – after winning the Alexandrian War alongside Cleopatra – a war he did not go to Egypt to engage in but recognized its opportunity – the two took a 3 month vacation along the Nile River

3 – Caesar and Cleopatra's relationship and alliance were both romantically and politically motivated; Caesar had come to Egypt chasing his vanquished adversary, Pompey. Arriving there, Caesar is dismayed to hear that Ptolemy, ruler and younger brother of Cleopatra, has killed Pompey, possibly to win Caesar's favor. The opposite occurred. In reaction to this (or maybe these were always his intentions and now he had political reason), Caesar aligns himself with Cleopatra in the siblings' ongoing feud. Likewise, Cleopatra sought out Caesar – who was now the most powerful man in Rome, and by extension, arguably with world – to aid her against Ptolemy. Historians dictate that not only was their romantic bond genuine and inexplicably passion-filled, but Caesar (and most probably Cleopatra as well) also saw future, dynastic opportunity between them, as sovereign rulers of power states forming a literal dynasty between them.

4 – *Poseidon*, Greek God of the Sea

5 – not a typo

If They Should Ask

If they should ask…

I will tell them…

that you and I were a well-made mojito poured over blood-
stained rocks, I will tell them that our love was the perfect
synergy of sanctity and sin:

I will tell them
that you and I were like gin and tonic on chronic,
that our style

of communication had me hooked up on your phonics,
I will tell them that you called me Onyx…

that I stepped
with boulders as big as clips on soldiers' hips and indeed, I
was hipped

to how you could dazzle, dip,
and swing low, and so

I called to your chariots in a tone

that was familiar to you because…

you know me…

I am that grip to which you surrender

all of your air,

I am the storm

that always seems to start around about your knees and travel

North,

I am that quiver

simply commanding that you accept,

the stair steps

to a heaven sanctioned unworthy

by the bearers of right and wrong,

and yet, I am the song you love

because you know no pair could rock to it with a rhythm

like ours,

I am your fears come true -

your most primal wants manifested in flesh,

I am the owner

of all your keys, the smith to all your locks,

the finder and re-designer of your *black box lost at sea* [1]...

the waterfalls to your forevers...

I was your thirst. You were my water,

and the worst thing that could have ever happened to either

of us

was that we found what we were looking for.

poem notes

---

1 – a device aboard an aircraft that audio records the flight for investigation purposes should the flight have an incident

Library at Alexandria

It is believed, though not unanimously agreed upon,
that the Library at Alexandria was largely incinerated as an
unintended consequence

of Caesar and Cleopatra's war against her younger Brother
and co-ruler, Ptolemy over supremacy of Egypt.

What is not up for debate is that undoubtedly, sacred
treasures, monuments of achievement, and all other accolades
of love and wonder are so very often torn asunder by the
inherent bludgeon and blunder of conquest.

Meanwhile, quests to satisfy unquenchable thirsts have
continuously led to the uprisings of all the worst sides within
all of us.

Combatants and non-combatants alike will all likely lose the
best of themselves in the wreck,

I myself have charred away the most tender parts of who I
was in pursuit of such fatal fantasies,

two-thousands years removed and yet the message behind the myth is more relevant than the question of its historical accuracy, the point is:

something always has to die in hot pursuit of dynasty;
and even our most victorious valuables can, and will all likely
be made victims in the aftermath. What they always fail to tell
you is that what you love

will always find a way to break you.

I've always wanted to be known as something more than just
another man who breaks things, yet

I've grown craftier in carnage than most men I know, and I
know there is no way of approximating the cost of the
damage inflicted upon the innocent, though

I suppose no market measurement can be assigned
to what is, by design, priceless, really all of what I am trying
to say is… I am sorry

for all the dust.

I am sorry. For the burdened memories of sacred texts. I am sorry for all the language lost. For all the incinerated poems, I am sorry. To every manuscript that has met a fiery end before its intended finish, I am aware

that apologies are unable to grow gardens at speeds comparable to which machetes are able chop them down or with the veracity flames take to crops,

reactionary by nature and futile in form,
apologies possess the least power of all

and I know

this cannot end with amends made…

I just miss the poems that I will never get to hear, and eternally mourn for all the futures that never were.

Burning and Looting

I greet the forest with a torch
and find calm in the flames.

I inhale the air and look for stairs
that will lead to locked doors. I pour

honey-mixed elixir on the knobs that sends
my liver into a riot, I quiet all the noise
with the burning
of the leaves.

I want everything
that's mine, and worse,
I want everything
that is yours.

Spare me the bore of simple things like peace.

I am here for every tear that you have invested
in tomorrow. I want your ceilings

on the floor and I know many ways to do it.
I am highly trained in the art of destruction, meaning

I am the sole reason why *massacre* and *masterpiece*
could ever be synonymous; one day,

I'll be a portrait on the wall of a boy that rises

every morning and stands before me, convinced
his inability to satiate himself justifies plunging the world into
a chaos and I hope

the fires in his belly don't fry away the nerves
that keep him human, meaning

I hope his need to feed his flames
doesn't leave him cold, meaning

I hope he knows when to stop….

burning and looting,
confusing destiny with addiction,

refusing to recognize that some stories aren't worth their

existence,

I hope he learns something from the destruction of

Alexandria's library. I hope it's clear

that the world shouldn't be the victim of Man's deathly desire

to play God, I hope he knows

having it all isn't worth the weight of all the world's sorrow,

more specifically

the sorrows of those who matter most,

I hope the ghosts don't find him, but

if I were the betting man that I am, I'd bet a stack of *sesterce* [1]

that they will,

and I'd double-down on a stack that I'll be burning still,

but hopefully, either dead,

or, at least, looting no longer.

poem notes

1 – a form of ancient Roman currency; a coin

Whatever

Today, I am whatever
the winds decide.

Today, I allow the leaves to deliver
the verdict, today

I am guilty.

Tonight I let the stars judge the honor
in my shine, tonight

I pine for boxing gloves and two-step
with my shadow, tonight

I take down the mountains
that once grew me legs and pour honey over my scars
to let the bees I know that we are not finished yet...

Tonight, tonight,
I wrestle wolves and howl at the Moon
until the Moon howls back,

tonight my newest name will be written

in the crops, tonight

we circle Truth and chant it ours

until we finally change its mind,

tonight…tonight…tonight

the escape has no plan, tonight

poet has no pen, and when Morning knocks

we will turn down the music just low enough

to say

Hello…how are you?

we will turn the music down just low enough

to make it clear

that we hope

it brought some sadness and poetry

of its own because we have none left to share…

we will turn down the music…

just low enough

to ask,

> *what more is a crown but dead weight?*
> *what more is height than the distance that you ultimately will*
> *fall?*

We will turn down the music just low enough
to shriek,

> *what is a plane without a pilot!*
> *What more is mite without soul than*
> *a fucking plane crash waiting to happen!*

We will turn the music down just low enough
to ask Morning who gave it its name.

> *Who the hell told it where to find us anyway!*

We will turn the music down just low enough
to ask Morning does it have a favorite song it'd like us to
spin,

We will turn the music down just low enough
to tell Morning

that whether it joins us or it jails us,

this will be the last time we ever turn down
the music again.

The Water's Edge

I fill my Hennessy to the brim with glass and
toast to the heavens.

I share a shot with the ground for those taken
at the expense of my tyranny and take a moment of silence,

how quick time fades.
How slow are we to reconcile
with reality.

What is the shelf life of a worn-down war dog?

How long do we have until the light inevitably checkmates us,
revealing

the battles beneath the skin?

How much more
will time consume us

until we realize

that all we are is a herd of broken clocks,
a stranded clan

of ticking time bombs
that all missed our detonations.

Truth is...I've accumulated more casualties than I ever

wanted. Truth is I can be named a traitor by some that would

have stopped at nothing for my betterment.

Maniacal behaviors at times have led me to be a maniac
and the majesty of no crown is strong enough to drown out
the pain, the indelible stains, the debris that remains, and yet I
stand here

at the water's edge,

searching for something more potent than power for my
powers to seek and pledge,

hoping to see something in the water beyond my own image,

imagining the taste of spring can bring about a beginning

strong enough to submerge the past in dirt,

knowing full well the earth only grows off the bones we

feed it. Truth is

I am not as I green

as I used to be, but

the Sun still rises, the waters

still recognize my soul, my glass is not yet empty,

and the chance to produce a self more pure is still as real

as the life I see

before me.

POPULARES

When the ambition of the individual aligns with the needs of the world in which he or she lives, all breathing are bound to benefit in the pursuit. Talents are for audiences. Goals are for accolades and personal power that feeds the wielder alone is power wasted. *Impact* answers if any of it mattered. To who? How?

Doubtlessly, throughout our lives we will extend our talents and power to misadventure, greed, glory, and personal acquisition (maybe even to our own downfalls); that is an assurance. Yet if we care to be recognized by history, is it with our impact that we must concern ourselves. *Impact* measures how who we are and what we do inspires and/or provides beyond ourselves, and this is what determines our legacy, the proof that we once existed.

Is there a cause greater than ourselves to which we have to commit our presence and capabilities? Of course there is. Plenty. One would argue: for what other reason are we provided with our unique sets of personality and skill-sets to be cultivated in the first place? Find it, that greater cause — your combination of avenues where you know you are of most influence and a contribution to progression - and find the start of your legacy.

The term *populares* refers to the political affiliation of the Late Roman Republic that campaigned for and aligned with social and political agendas that were more democratic, "popular causes" concerned with the Republic as a whole, specifically the many thousands of Romans who possessed the least – the marginalized. Conversely, the *optimates* were the politicians who advocated for a more conservative agenda that favored "the best" of Romans – the elite.

Caesar is arguably the most beloved and celebrated populares of the Roman Republic, but he is just one of a long line before him who were also assassinated – not for their "thirst for power", "tyrannical behaviors", or "insatiable desire for bloodletting" (in fact, Caesar's career-long habit of forgiveness, clemency, and reconciliation is incomparable to any other Roman leader of the Late Republic), but for his desire to provide relief to Rome's impoverished citizens and what these reliefs would mean for the rich and powerful few who had enjoyed lives of generational luxury, often under the leadership of consuls far more tyrannical and threatening to the Roman way of life than Caesar ever was, could have been, or desired to be, but were aligned with reactionary agendas that reinforced the status quo – a status quo that robbed, preyed upon, and victimized its financially/socially-vulnerable citizens. For sure, revenge was also a driving motivator in the assassination plot, as many of the conspirators were of the defeated faction of the civil war in which Caesar was the victor, yet they were pardoned and welcomed back to the Senate (though political tradition accepted that these defeated men be put to death, but Caesar was known for his clemency and political forgiveness – surely, a tactic often times applied for his own political gain, inspiring (or demanding coercing) from his former-foes who would now owe him their lives.

It is said that during one of Caesar's last suppers, while talking about death with his closest lieutenants and associates – including Marc Atony, his closest soldier and right-hand man, as well as Decimus, also a once-loyal lieutenant who would also be the conspirator that would lead Caesar out of his home and towards his bloody demise the morning of *The Ides of March* – that he preferred a quick and sudden end as oppose to a death that was arduous and toilsome. Irony would have that *Caesar's luck* (a term inspired by his knack for getting/creating his own desired outcome via how he applied his will and force to circumstances) would again prevail. Just days later, headed into a Senate meeting that his wife Calpurnia begged him not to attend, the beloved Roman hero, who was a king in all but name, was knifed to death by roughly two dozen of his colleagues.

Now, none of us can know when our own *Ides of March* will arrive. Yet once we begin to examine our potential for creating *impact* – which begins with a journey of self-reflection and discovery – we are ready to begin our life's work – securing and establishing our legacy.

A Soothsayer's Promise

Woke up this morning -
a new, green moon in my eyes.

Intentions locked on matters set to maximize
until my inevitable demise…

I house books along my window sills like plants set for
sunlight and wonder off in search of the accompanying
metaphor in the distance.

Running a clean rag along the spines of each, I am pulled into
flashbacks of which I have never lived yet still remember all
too well.

I am suddenly an a legionnaire chiseling his sword with a
forest rock, I am a marksman nurturing his rifles. Truthfully,

I am a disciple of controversial folks.

Most of my heroes have known violence and many of them
were, once or maybe even twice, the perpetrator.

An agitated and agitating academic myself,

an opportunist awaiting to unveil the future in his poems, and

a love for home that wasn't built in a day, I have converted

my living room into a bunker.

I hold an arsenal on my tongue. No, this trip will not remind

you of *Nirvana* [1]. There will be no *Pax Romana* [2] until the *plebs*

[3] have their piece, so release this statement to the press:

Rest is for the satiated.

So it may be anticipated that you will not see sleep until the

reckoning is complete, until Rome knows a New Day,

until the wicked pay for their violations, until

the constellations can confirm that they can hear us,

trust,

you would be wise to believe me. Consider this a

soothsayers promise [4]. A word for the woke.

I hope you heard.

End poem.

poem notes

---

1 - In Hinduism and Buddhism, *nirvana* is the highest state of consciousness that someone can attain, a state of enlightenment,

2 – pax romana – as its name implies – was a 200 year period of relative peace and prosperity in Rome and the surrounding region, beginning towards the end of August's reign; partial reason for this period of peace is that all of the region would fall under Roman law

3 – the plebeian class, often referred to as "plebs", were the commoner/low class of Rome

4 – a soothsayer is someone thought to be able to channel divine messages or have foresight of the future. Spurinna is the name of the soothsayer, who was also politically connected to the anti-Caesar elite, who warned Caesar of his impending assassination.

In Celebration of a Fatal Baptism

(Republished from 2016's chapbook, *In Celebration of a Fatal Baptism*)

My block was named after a slave master.

I've lived, and hurt, here for years and yet my tears

fall to the ground with a hopelessness

synonymous to the sound of nails

piercing

innocent hands.

As I stand here…

I hold the weight and hear

the whispers of a thousand dead poets

with stories like mine and in time were all forgotten,

their words too rotten with honesty for the anthologies that

told them *no*.

As I laugh

I grow cold, recalling Langston,

his verse – the *Darker Brother* [1] – and I wonder

what part of me made me the Dark matter

that never mattered,

and so I've groomed myself a Son

of Sun people – my pen writing

me out of pinstripes

and into *Adinkra symbols* [2],

panthers screaming the slogans etched

into my forearms, their paws covering my chest,

charging me with jargons.

My body…

My body now a mausoleum

      written in hope and hieroglyphs

so the eulogy reads of

bleak,

    beautiful,

        Blackness.

Massa may own the block

but he don't own me.

 I baptize in this Blackness,

this hereditary tar

and if I swim out too far

and I drown beneath the weight of the chains,

know

that these were the chains I chose,
and not those

hanging

from the street signs.

‘

poem notes

---

1 – a reference to a line from the poem "I, Too" by Langston Hughes

2 – African symbols that represent communicate spirituality and other divine principles

Proscriptions 1: A Love Letter to Black Bodies

Black bodies…

Black bodies for your fields,

Black bodies for your labor.

Black bodies dissolved into a melting pot,

and served to spice up your American flavor.

Black bodies for best sellers.

Black bodies for your box office hits.

Black bodies for ballot boxes,

Black bodies for your soapbox stanzas,

Black bodies for your campaign cause,

Black bodies

for your laws to ignore.

Black bodies for target practice.

Black bodies for target practice.

Black bodies for target practice.

Black bodies for the penalty of breathing,
Black bodies for your seething hate,
Black bodies for your torture, castration and rape.

Black bodies for your HOT 9-7 jam of the week.
Black bodies forever paving the way towards the
righteousness you seek and preach,

black bodies
for your favorite sport, black bodies to hang
hundreds and hundreds of years on in court.

Black bodies for your poster-boards and postcards,
Black bodies for your police.

Black bodies for your feast.
Please, Black bodies for you to eat, your treat, please

thirst no longer. Be frail no more. Sop up the blood with a
biscuit. *Wash it down with willful apathy
and live in star-spangled bliss.*

The dawn's early light never shines on black bodies…

except only to pillage the remains…

Black bodies…

outlined,   *redlined* [1],

stream-lined,   pipe- lined,

piped down,   piped up,

strung up,   fleeced down,

masqueraded,

paraded through the streets like prisoners of war,
lined up, walled in

by more and more and more and more
black bodies…

all the names…all the bones…

a master's dwelling, all the privilege and all the precious
stones…payloads, endorsement deals, political platforms,
reconstitutions of all the norms, all the power we employ, all
the tragedy you enjoy…

I guess we all owe *Othello* [1] a box of Cubans…
Should send *Ricky's mother* [2] a couple of royalty checks,

tattoo the names of those slain for us to have a reason to say
utter a word across our tongues,

fill our lunges with the ashes of *Crispis Atticks* [3],
and make sure our markets are ready
for more and more black bodies.

poem notes

---

1 – refers to *redlining,* the discriminatory practice of systemically segregating and denying Black Americans from housing opportunities after the Depression

2 – the tragic play written by Shakespeare that centers around an outsider – a Black man who is also a ranking soldier – in the Italian city of Venice; Othello is driven to murder-suicide in this play about jealousy and "otherness"

3 – a fictional character of the movie Boyz In the Hood, whose son is murdered

4 – a Black man and the first casualty in what would become the American Revolutionary War

Proscriptions 2: An Incomplete List

#BreonnaTaylor #BreonnaTaylor #BreonnaTaylor
#BreonnaTaylor #BreonnaTaylor #BreonnaTaylor
#BreonnaTaylor #BreonnaTaylor #BreonnaTaylor

#SandraBland #SandraBland #SandraBland
#SandraBland #SandraBland #SandraBland
#SandraBland #SandraBland #SandraBland

#YvetteSmith #YvetteSmith #YvetteSmith
#YvetteSmith #YvetteSmith #YvetteSmith
#YvetteSmith #YvetteSmith #YvetteSmith

#ShereeseFrancis #ShereeseFrancis #ShereeseFrancis
#ShereeseFrancis #ShereeseFrancis #ShereeseFrancis
#ShereeseFrancis #ShereeseFrancis #ShereeseFrancis

#AuraRosser #AuraRosser #AuraRosser
#AuraRosser #AuraRosser #AuraRosser
#AuraRosser #AuraRosser #AuraRosser

#KendreaJames #KendreaJames #KendreaJames

\#KendreaJames \#KendreaJames \#KendreaJames
\#KendreaJames \#KendreaJames \#KendreaJames

\#LatanyaHaggerty \#LatanyaHaggerty \#LatanyaHaggerty
\#LatanyaHaggerty \#LatanyaHaggerty \#LatanyaHaggerty
\#LatanyaHaggerty \#LatanyaHaggerty \#LatanyaHaggerty

\#AiyanaStanleyJones \#AiyanaStanleyJones
\#AiyanaStanleyJones \#AiyanaStanleyJones
\#AiyanaStanleyJones \#AiyanaStanleyJones
\#AiyanaStanleyJones \#AiyanaStanleyJones

\#TanishaAnderson \#TanishaAnderson \#TanishaAnderson
\#TanishaAnderson \#TanishaAnderson \#TanishaAnderson
\#TanishaAnderson \#TanishaAnderson \#TanishaAnderson

\#AtatianaJefferson \#AtatianaJefferson \#AtatianaJefferson
\#AtatianaJefferson \#AtatianaJefferson \#AtatianaJefferson
\#AtatianaJefferson \#AtatianaJefferson \#AtatianaJefferson

\#CharleenaLyles \#CharleenaLyles \#CharleenaLyles
\#CharleenaLyles \#CharleenaLyles \#CharleenaLyles
\#CharleenaLyles \#CharleenaLyles \#CharleenaLyles

#KorrynGaines #KorrynGaines #KorrynGaines
#KorrynGaines #KorrynGaines #KorrynGaines
#KorrynGaines #KorrynGaines #KorrynGaines

#MyaHall #MyaHall #MyaHall
#MyaHall #MyaHall #MyaHall
#MyaHall #MyaHall #MyaHall

#ElaonorBumpurs #ElaonorBumpurs #ElaonorBumpurs
#ElaonorBumpurs #ElaonorBumpurs #ElaonorBumpurs
#ElaonorBumpurs #ElaonorBumpurs #ElaonorBumpurs

#MeaganHockaday #MeaganHockaday #MeaganHockaday
#MeaganHockaday #MeaganHockaday #MeaganHockaday
#MeaganHockaday #MeaganHockaday

#JanishaFonville #JanishaFonville #JanishaFonville
#JanishaFonville #JanishaFonville #JanishaFonville
#JanishaFonville #JanishaFonville #JanishaFonville

#NatahaMcKenna #NatahaMcKenna #NatahaMcKenna
#NatahaMcKenna #NatahaMcKenna #NatahaMcKenna
#NatahaMcKenna #NatahaMcKenna #NatahaMcKenna

#ShenequeProctor #ShenequeProctor #ShenequeProctor
#ShenequeProctor #ShenequeProctor #ShenequeProctor
#ShenequeProctor #ShenequeProctor #ShenequeProctor
#MichelleCusseaux #MichelleCusseaux #MichelleCusseaux
#MichelleCusseaux #MichelleCusseaux #MichelleCusseaux

#PearlieGolden #PearlieGolden #PearlieGolden
#PearlieGolden #PearlieGolden #PearlieGolden
#PearlieGolden #PearlieGolden #PearlieGolden

#GabriellaNevarez #GabriellaNevarez #GabriellaNevarez
#GabriellaNevarez #GabriellaNevarez #GabriellaNevarez
#GabriellaNevarez #GabriellaNevarez #GabriellaNevarez

#MiriamCarey #MiriamCarey #MiriamCarey #MiriamCarey
#MiriamCarey #MiriamCarey #MiriamCarey #MiriamCarey
#MiriamCarey #MiriamCarey #MiriamCarey #MiriamCarey

#KyamLivingston #KyamLivingston #KyamLivingston
#KyamLivingston #KyamLivingston #KyamLivingston
#KyamLivingston #KyamLivingston #KyamLivingston

#KaylaMoore #KaylaMoore #KaylaMoore #KaylaMoore
#KaylaMoore #KaylaMoore #KaylaMoore #KaylaMoore
#KaylaMoore #KaylaMoore #KaylaMoore #KaylaMoore

#ShellyFrey #ShellyFrey #ShellyFrey #ShellyFrey
#ShellyFrey #ShellyFrey #ShellyFrey #ShellyFrey
#ShellyFrey #ShellyFrey #ShellyFrey #ShellyFrey
#ShellyFrey #ShellyFrey #ShellyFrey #ShellyFrey

#MalissaWilliams #MalissaWilliams #MalissaWilliams
#MalissaWilliams #MalissaWilliams #MalissaWilliams
#MalissaWilliams #MalissaWilliams #MalissaWilliams

#AlesiaThomas #AlesiaThomas #AlesiaThomas
#AlesiaThomas #AlesiaThomas #AlesiaThomas
#AlesiaThomas #AlesiaThomas #AlesiaThomas

#ShantelDavis #ShantelDavis #ShantelDavis #ShantelDavis
#ShantelDavis #ShantelDavis #ShantelDavis #ShantelDavis
#ShantelDavis #ShantelDavis #ShantelDavis #ShantelDavis

\#TarikaWilson \#TarikaWilson \#TarikaWilson

\#TarikaWilson \#TarikaWilson \#TarikaWilson

\#TarikaWilson \#TarikaWilson \#TarikaWilson

\#KathrynJohnston \#KathrynJohnston \#KathrynJohnston

\#KathrynJohnston \#KathrynJohnston \#KathrynJohnston

\#KathrynJohnston \#KathrynJohnston \#KathrynJohnston

\#AlbertaSpruill \#AlbertaSpruill \#AlbertaSpruill

\#AlbertaSpruill \#AlbertaSpruill \#AlbertaSpruill

\#AlbertaSpruill \#AlbertaSpruill \#AlbertaSpruill

\#MargaretLaverneMitchell \#MargaretLaverneMitchell

\#MargaretLaverneMitchell \#MargaretLaverneMitchell

\#MargaretLaverneMitchell \#MargaretLaverneMitchell

\#MargaretLaverneMitchell \#MargaretLaverneMitchell

\#TyishaMiller \#TyishaMiller \#TyishaMiller \#TyishaMiller

\#TyishaMiller \#TyishaMiller \#TyishaMiller \#TyishaMiller

\#TyishaMiller \#TyishaMiller \#TyishaMiller \#TyishaMiller

#DannetteDaniels #DannetteDaniels #DannetteDaniels
#DannetteDaniels #DannetteDaniels #DannetteDaniels
#DannetteDaniels #DannetteDaniels #DannetteDaniels

#FrankieAnnPerkins #FrankieAnnPerkins
#FrankieAnnPerkins #FrankieAnnPerkins
#FrankieAnnPerkins #FrankieAnnPerkins
#FrankieAnnPerkins #FrankieAnnPerkins

#SonjiTaylor #SonjiTaylor #SonjiTaylor
#SonjiTaylor #SonjiTaylor #SonjiTaylor
#SonjiTaylor #SonjiTaylor #SonjiTaylor

"Proscription" lists were the lists of names of Roman Citizens declared condemned by the State. The people on these lists were now bounties for all citizens; fellow Romans were rewarded for finding and slaying these condemned individuals, often time receiving handsome reward for their service. The possessions of the slain would become the property of the State. Political agitation, xenophobia, being affiliated with the wrong class, or having something treasured by the State are all but some of the reasons your name could be on the next list. The names of the Black Women – the American Citizens – used here is done in respect and honor to their memory and as a reminder of how some of our worst practices, 2000 years later, are still with us.

This Poem Is Important

It is important that I write about Black women,

it is important that I write about Black women,

it is important that I write about Black women,

it is important that I write about Black women because…

my mother's first name is Patricia.

It is important that I write about Black women,

It is important that I write about Black women,

It is important that I write about Black women because…

God demands: **honor me in all my glory.**

It is important that I write about Black women, because

at no time in human history have Black women not been

important,

creators, captains, the cause, the cure,

held captive, conspired against, counted out, left unaccounted

for, confined, hell…

anywhere in the world a Black woman smiles, she is
demonstrating an act of protest…It is important

that I write about Black women.
It is important that I write about Black women,
It is important that I write about Black women because…

my story, or any story, told with the absence of Black women
is a story incomplete, or in other words, **a lie.**

It is important that I write about Black women because
in 24 b.c. Kandake Amanirenas – Queen of the Kushite
Empire – skillfully and successfully lead her soldiers in
resistance to Roman aggression and despite History's War
Campaign against Black Women a Queen's power will always
rise from the oppression that attempts to drown her,

it is important…
that I write about Black Women.

It is important that I write about Black Women,
it is important that I write about Black Women, because…

I love them, because I have written poems inspired by the pain I have inflicted upon Black women,

because I, too, have been a conspirator against them with my silence, it is important that I write about Black women because

my Mother's first name is Patricia,

her last name is a city in Italy and though she has never been there is no necessary reason to even have to put *because* after *why it is important that I write about Black women*, nor should the world need further explanation on why Black women are important, and should be written about, and read about, and listened to. Can't you see?

I write about Black women not because Patricia Florence and *Aurelia Cotta* [1] would make fine friends, but because I don't understand how the words *mother* and *messiah* are not synonyms.

It is important that I write about Black women because everything I can say about Patricia, I've been told about God, yet she is no different from every Black woman I have ever known or read about. And so,

it is important that I write about Black women.

poem notes

---

1 - Aurelia Cotta is the name of Caesar's mother

Patricia Florence

Shamara Larkins

Ja'Najah Larkins

Elu Catori & Ya'Nae Brown

Robin Frierson

Naimah Dematra Wallace

Mariah Alston

Jolan Browne

Jawariah Raheem & Dayana Poulard

Ameerah Shabazz-Bilal

Ann Frierson

Succession

Earlier in his career, while holding a political office in Spain,
Caesar, aged roughly

in his thirties,

is said to have visited upon a statue
of Alexander the 3rd of Macedon,

(commonly referred to as Alexander The Great).

Legend has it, the sight of Alexander –

a young man who had lived 200 years earlier, inherited an
empire, expanded that empire across three continents, and
merged Eastern and Western cultures and was dead by the
age Caesar was as he gazed upon this statue of his hero –

brought Caesar to tears, dismayed

at how much he had not done in the same span of years it
had taken his idol to conquer the "known world".

A fascinating tale of fate,

how if we connect the dots without mistake,

that I can tell a similar story between myself and a man

who fashioned himself

Nipsey Tha Great.

Nip…I salute you, General. I'm sure Alexander

would do the same as we marvel at how you bought game to

the block, and gangstas to the boardroom,

how you broke bread with the babies,

employed they mamas and daddies on the same streets you

used to hustle,

how you led with mind over muscle but wouldn't hesitate to

activate arms when the alarms sounded,

how you pounded pavement and perception in the direction

of a greater good and higher truth…

how you turned the booth into a lecture hall, influenced

goons to practice more God talk between them.

I don't know the qualifications for a Saint, Nip,

but I know you ain't nothing less than such in my hood,

nothing less than a prophet in my home,

and so I rally and roam through the streets bearing your face

on my shirt when it is time to go to work.

I practice alchemy making moments into marathons while

chanting down Babylon knowing that *God will rise* [1] and when

the tides have finally shifted…

and the tax for being Black has been lifted…

and the good, graceful and gifted are all gathered to dance

and glorify themselves under the protection of Destiny...

It will be me ensuring that the world recognizes your

contribution to the recipe…

I dedicate whatever is left of me to the *Marathon* [2]

and until I reach the checkered flag, you can tell the Big

Homie, I got it from here…

poem notes

1 – *God will rise* is the meaning of slain musician, entrepreneur, and activist Nipsey Hussle's birth name, Ermias.

2 – reference to Nipsey's album titles and trademark slogan, The Marathon Continues

#MY STUDENTS
ARE WATCHING

STOP
POLICE
TERROR
Here Because
MY STUDENTS
ARE WATCHING
LOVE to LEARN
LEARN to LIVE
RUN
DMC

STOP
POLICE
BRUTALITY
NO JUSTICE
NO PEACE
BLACK
LIVES
MATTER

Letters: To The Legions (Can't Stop, Won't Stop)

I grew up, living life

like it was *me against the world*. Anticipating

the day I would stand in front of it, with

all eyez on me,

I

wanted to be a Young *Pac*

to my peers, promising the populace

that if they lent me their eyes would provide

the *blueprint* on how to get *paid, in full,*

Ha! Full of shit, I was…

Full of shit I was for thinking,

thinking

I had the *juice,*

thinking

I was built for *Cuban Links* on brink of something big

until the jig was up!

Until the *Clubber Lang's* of the game
stepped in the ring to reveal how *rocky* the road gets,
I mean…shit!

I *pity the fool* I was for my charade, parading
to be a *prince* among peasants as if I knew why *doves cry,*

a *little child running* with wild *cashmere thoughts* of being *Superfly,*

doing *Bad Boy shit – Notorious like B.I.,*

but see, *Real G's,* they schooled me real quick –
natty heads with ganja spliffs the size
of cigar sticks singing *songs of redemption* cleared up the vision

in my Far Eye, and now?....Now?

Well…as far as I can see…as far as I can see
the prophecy is clear!

From Jersey to *Jamrock*, I know the Exodus is near! *Welcome to the terror dome*! Open your mind and see what is really going on!

Clap your hands and stop your feet as we *chant down Babylon*, you see…

the world is a *ball of confusion,*
temptations are everywhere.

I said the world is a *ball of confusion,*
temptations are everywhere!

Rolling stones lead to broken homes and *butterflies get pimped* for dreaming of wanting more. I say it's time to settle *the score*!

Ready or not, the plot is coming!

Everybody loves the sunshine but idle minds are quickly *hypnotized* and before you know it,

they'll have you thinking *revolutions can be televised,* I tell no lies! In fact, I pray that *you forget me not*!

A hotboy! A buffalo soldier! Dreadlock Rasta! Impostas are broken

off proppa, *who shot ya!?*

Probably the police I'm sure, how they kick in the door,

WAVINGGG *the FOUR-FOUR!*

Fred Hampton! Fred Hampton style is how they wild on *homies*

and thugs like us, but

question is will you buss back?

Bullet, ballot, sword, or word, how will you see to it that you

are heard?

When the night has come, will you run or remain still?

When the land is dark, will you spark up something other than a

bag of loud? I mean,

will your seeds be proud to say they grow from you?

Are you really *ready to die*, beyond a *reasonable doubt,*
for what you believe? *Dear Mama…*

*if I die tonight…*I pray you leave the casket open!

Picture me rollin' with every other Rebel laid down, now in
Thugz Mansion for saying something that really mattered…

Gather all the folks from the past and blast all the tunes I
crooned in hard times, play every song that kept me sane,

rock out to all the rhythms and blues that speak the truth,
pleasure, and pains about being Black, bold, and bound to
make a difference.

Let everyone witness that even in my death, *today was a good
day* for us. Because true soldiers…they NEVER die!

Their spirits live forever in the people they inspire! Raptured
in the *whispers, the beat goes on*!

And on! And on! And on!

The protests never rest. The record keep spinning, so let the
record show, and LET THE WORLD KNOW,
That we

CAN'T STOP, WON'T STOP,

CAN'T STOP, WON'T STOP!

There IS no choice! We ARE one voice! So let us rejoice and
celebrate how we've come so far, because

every nigga is a star,
in my opinion!

From *King Kunta* to Mansa Musa,
from corner block to Capitol Hill,
from plantation to president,

from *Hell bound* to *Heaven Sent*

its been forever lit over here!

So keep your head up, and your shields too,

because we've proven time and time again that there is

nothing we cannot do.

YOU!

Cream of the crop, *keep rising*

to the top…

and while you're at it, be sure you let them know…

That we

CAN'T STOP! WON'T STOP!

       CAN'T STOP! WON'T STOP!

poem notes

---

* each italicized phrase of this poem is either a reference to a song or album title, a song lyric, a musician/musical group, or a popular American movie

** Fred Hampton was a rising and ranking member of the Black Panther Party for Self Defense – an organization founded upon the self-reliant and self-defense philosophies of Malcolm X. The Panthers provided neighborhood security, education courses, and meal services amongst other works for Black communities across the 1970s before its infiltration by the FBI.

Fred Hampton, aged 21, was murdered at 4am by government agents as his apartment was raided and he slept in bed, drugged.

COMMENTARIES

History – the collected accounts of past events – will always be written with, and therefore contain, the biases, intentions, and judgement of its writers. That said, every recorded act of our lives – should they be entered into "history" - will have inherent inaccuracies accounts. Likewise, the dead cannot demand retractions. Therefore, the power of being responsible for the authorship of your own life is of unquantifiable importance.

Recognizing this during the first year of his governorship in Gaul – too far physically removed from Rome to hold the influence he would otherwise been able to maintain while physically there – Caesar began writing yearly reports of he and his army's encounters, battles, and victories abroad. Written in the 3rd person (Caesar never refers to himself as "I" but as "Caesar"), these accounts kept Caesar and the progression of his mission on Rome's behalf (and, seemingly at times, his own behalf) on the minds of everyday citizens and the Senate alike. These collected reports are known as *The Commentaries: On the Gallic War*.

Reading these accounts of Roman conquest, victory, adventure, and the exploration of "fantastical lands" beyond

Rome engendered loyalty and favor with most Roman commoners and provided them a faraway hero in Caesar and his army for which to root. Surely, Caesar was sharp enough to recognize and take advantage of this ability to write his own propaganda to better ensure a successful run for his 2nd consulship once done with his governorship. What he may not have been aware of was that, by writing his own story in his own words, today we know more about the person of Caesar – his personality, intentions, and ambitions – than we know of most individuals of antiquity comparably.

We cannot know if he expected that these reports would survive antiquity and be the foundational texts in the study of Latin today that they have become, but regardless of Caesar's intention, this consequence speaks to just how important it is that we not only be the authors of our stories via our intentional actions, but our intentional word in reference to those actions. For course, those set to manipulate your work and words will always find their avenues to do so, but having no choice but to also address a subject's own commentary on their own matters better strengthens and guards the subject's intention and integrity from slander because the subject's own analysis cannot be avoided in the overall analysis.

Point being: leave as little space as possible for misinterpretation, unintended or otherwise, about who you are, why you are, and what you are doing, by setting the record straight yourself. Be more than the protagonist of your story, be its principal author and documentarian. State what happened. Capture it yourself. Give others no choice but to face your reality as they collect their own on who you are and what you stand for. The clarity you provide on you is essential. Ensure your truth is recorded. Not every utterance is meant to ease, but truth is its own reward and the record of your truth will live long beyond your exit. It may possible even become a springboard or lighthouse in the development of those who will be fortunate enough to make contact with it in the future.

Wings

Hands, heavy
with the weight of my decisions,

Life, filled
with the conquests on my ambitions,

I wonder…

I wonder
if this is what it means to strive…

To place one foot in front of the next and step upon the
ledge as if the air has arms stretched, just waiting to reward
me

for my desire to fly, though truthfully...
truthfully, I don't know why I want wings…

I can't decide my reason for wanting to rival the birds.

Maybe, it is to know what it feels like to be weightless.

Maybe it is to be assured that I am a burden no longer.

Maybe it is to remind myself that I am one with the clouds,

maybe, I have just convinced myself that I have earned my
right to breathe air!

Maybe Oxygen and I have a bond I can't explain!

Maybe flight is all I know! Maybe elevation is my only
address,

maybe, I am not meant to come down,

maybe, the winds have other plans for me…

HOPEFULLY. Hopefully
the day I finally touch down I can die happy to have written
such poems…

Happy
to have lived life in altitude.

Happy
to have seen and known turbulence.

Happy

to have tumbled and tussled with the whirlwinds. Happy

to have seen eye to eye with the tornadoes, I hope…

I hope the sky cracks and the rains fall

the day I'm ushered to the dirt.

I hope the soil can understand how

even in death I remain one with the elements.

I hope that I sleep tight.

That I might find my place amongst the gravel.

That the stones may look upon me and see kin.

That I might be considered food for both

the minerals and the memories.

Remembered consistently for the chaos,

for the magic and the madness,

for the words like liquid and the poems like wings,

the one who sang of things like love,

the one who told you straight lines didn't exist.

He

who couldn't resist the temptation of the clouds,

He

who told you to LIVE LOUD.

To be bold in how you step,
and be sure you rep for the ones who too desire higher
heights;

I humbly ask that you might consider me your pilot…

But, be sure that you are securely strapped in
as this flight will not be interrupted just because you are not
ready.

This aerial caravan
will never give a DAMN about whether or not you are
scared, and besides…

how can one really say they've lived life without knowing the
full thrill of uncertainty?

How could anyone be sure of anything without exploring the
unknown?

I guess this is why I
find home amongst the birds…

Maybe the rivalry between us is but a familiar, competitive
passion for soaring above the sensible and mundane…

Maybe we both share a love for stretching out limbs in order
to be guided by the gods as we look down, scoffing at
conventional wisdom…

laughing at what the world told us we ought be…

forever elated that the shackles that grow from barren lands
could never ascend high enough

to catch us by our ankles…
and determined…

determined to live life as both a whisper in the wind and a
roaring reminder that freedom

is nothing

if not the genuine belief that we humans,

too,

have the ability

to fly.

Letters: to the Senate

Your labelling of me as the enemy is a lie.

You would like nothing more than to advertise me as an agitator intent on destroying, and yet paradoxically there is truth in that…

Because the truth is…
there is poison in the water.

The truth is there is hate manufactured
in the air we breathe, truth is

the status quo has always been but a knee to my neck that has only left me alive long enough to prove to me how many more bodies it can strangle before it sends me to sleep,

the truth is

the status quo is a hand that has been pillaging my pockets since before I was able to fit rompers, the truth is…the truth is

that the truth has never really mattered to you;
it pales in your priority to keep the hold you have upon the
herd, and the truth is we have all seen, heard, and had enough
of the hypocrisy,

I am not, myself, a holy man. *Pontifex Maximus* [1] aside,
inside my heart's chamber resides unspeakable regrets,
the heavy weights of debts I could never repay,

and words that chew away at my organs in anger over my
inability to say them,

yet make no mistake, I am no monster and my legions will
not allow your attempt to spin a truth teller into a tyrant.

If…I am hell-bent on destroying today, it is because today
has never been a kind day for my kind and if

this fight is but a reminder to you that your wickedness will
not be met without resistance,

then I insist you keep your hand in the reach of your weapon,
I insist that you keep your words within the bounds of
recognition of my power, because me and my kind are ready
to remind you.

This is no intentional threat. This is no declaration of war,
but I implore that you recognize that *I am the Rubicon itself.*

I am that pivotal point of no return. Yesterday is gone. Let it rest,

or prepare yourself a pillow

next to it, your citizens are dying. Your tax payers are hungry.
Soon your property and prestige will be all that is left to feast
upon,

I write this warning in the highest order of honest love

to ensure that there is pure honor in the air
tomorrow when we meet at the battle lines.

I hope to see you ready. I hope you prove yourselves more
than oligarchs with nothing more but oration to offer,

I hope to see you and yours side by side at dawn

with rods of fearlessness firmly planted strong within your

spines,

I hope the grip around your gladius is too tight to entertain

doubt,

I hope you mark your routes with care and believe in your

strategy like you believe in my ability to carve history out of

my opposition, the point is…

that, like it or not, yesterday is dead. I AM the Rubicon.

As for tomorrow?

Hell only knows…

poem notes

---

1 - Pontifex Maximus was the title of the chief priest over the official priesthood branches of Roman. Caesar held at a young age, an achievement for such a prestigious office

Letters: to Brutus

Dear *Brutus* [1],

I understand why I have to die.

Dear Brutus,

we don't have the time for me to ask you why,

besides, Dear Brutus I'm sure

Mother confided in you well,

Dear Brutus,

please tell her that I love her still. Tell her my last sentiments

to you in this moment. Tell her how I told you to ensure that

you

die a legend, die a leader,

die living,

die never allowing for death to find you waiting for it,

die with your destiny assured.

Die in defiance.

Die letting the daggers know they failed; impale you, they can.
Replace you they cannot. Someone beneath my fortitude,
Brutus, would petition the gods that you rot

in hell for what you've done but, no, not I, Brutus.
I know how death robs you from life's burden,

I want you to carry this with you, Brutus. Through the sands
you encounter I want you to carry this. Across the deserts,
Brutus, learn from the mirages that seek your sanity; guard
your humanity from the ghosts, Brutus, take notes on all the
methods they pursue in hot pursuit to destroy you.

Brutus, I hope you lead a mighty chase.

I hope you see my face at night Brutus.
I hope you look back on today with nothing
but pride,

I hope I died leaving behind something for you to teach your
children, Brutus I hope you tell them how you knew me. Tell
them why you knew me and why I had to die. Tell them our

whole story. Tell them how you choose blood for what you called righteous sake, Brutus

I hope you are awake when the bell tolls.

When the tide rolls in your direction, I hope you are as lucky enough as I am to have someone you love doing you the honor.

Brutus I hope you forever hold your honor high, I hope you take it with you to the grave, Brutus.

I hope you sleep well. Sleep well. Sleep well, Brutus. I hope you sleep well.

Sleep well.

poem notes

---

1 – Marcus Brutus was a Roman politician of noble lineage. He was the son of Servilia, a socially and politically influential woman who was also a longtime and important lover of Caesar. Formally an ally of Caesar who then sided with Pompey during the Civil War, Caesar's personal affection for Brutus is how and why he survived losing the war, nor was he ever significantly injured during the war, at Caesar's request.

It is unclear if Brutus was a lead conspirator in the plot, but his involvement in the murder reportedly shocked Caesar in his last moments.

Letters: to The Daggers

You've wanted my body for years.

You've waited to see me finally beneath you,
I hope it hardens your manhood.

I hope the sight of me stiffens you.

I hope you run home and are swiftly given a hero's welcome
by your slaves and significant others.

I want you to know I condone your rejoicing. Live it up
before the riots break. I hope you have a plan

for your escape; many will be awaiting you.

In your hot pursuit for the boarder I hope you savor a
moment to watch how the streets rally for their son. Get a
glimpse of what sort of homage a city gives a soldier.

Awaiting my train ride to hell...I consider all the

things I'll be sure to tell the devil when I get there (besides beginning with how it's about time he finally got the fucking heat fixed).

I'll be sure to let him know to make space for more coming from where I came from.

It's a pity I won't be able to address the people that crowd my corpse and applaud them for coming out tonight. I wish I could hear Dante's *speech* [1].

Your victory in my death will be your last until Death himself *doubles back* [2].

I was sure to share with him an express route.

Told him to look for the ones I kept him from just some years ago,

he reminded me that real always recognizes real, and so he hasn't forgotten a single face.

I've cleared a space for us to shoot dice when you get here.

Just remember that you owe me one and this time…

I am intend to collect.

poem notes

---

1 – Dante refers to artist and chief consigliere of Ras Heru, Dante Ebron. Here, Dante is standing in for Marc Atony, who gave a rousing speech at Caesar's impromptu pyre funeral the night of the morning he was assassinated.

2 – The assassins, who had no real plan for government or the people post-assassination, recognized on the night of the pyre – the same day Caesar – that the people had not approved off their deed. The rallying of the Roman people that night, further galvanized by Marc Atony's speech, persuaded the conspirators to pack and leave Rome soon as they could. They did, and soon would see war against Atony, Octavian, and the rest of Caesar's supporters. These conspirators would all lose and die in the ensuring civil war into which they had plunged Rome.

The Rubicon: Epilogue/A Final Decree

I AM the Rubicon.

And so are you.

YOU are the Rubicon. Be that unique presence and force in the lives of everyone blessed to have your audience that they now cannot avoid having to account for. Be unavoidable. Maximize your impression. Be so that they have no choice but to take inventory in a manner that recognizes you and your contribution to their reality.

What else is the Rubicon?

Each waking day you have. Each day you are fortunate enough to rise, you have *crossed* into a world you must now face, as you can never go back.

What will be written about your crossing? What decisions are you willing to commit yourself to, and how well are they aligned with the expansion of your impact, value, and happiness?

You are powerful. You ARE power.

Watch your step. It will be recorded.

Acknowledgements

The Rubicon was a collective effort. Special love and acknowledgements to:

- Editor, forward writer and friend Ameerah Shabazz-Bilal

- Illustrator and friend Dayana Poulard

- Photographer and friend Matt Pierce

- And all the other Black women that have inspired and/or supported *The Rubicon*.

About the Author

Ras Heru Stewart is a Newark, NJ. born poet, artist, creative entrepreneur and elementary school teacher. Ras Heru's poems are ongoing conversations and explorations into the cores of the things that drive people. His poems are reflective and commanding, observant and self-assured yet meek and always pondering.

Executive producer of *Rhythm & Words: Creative Writing* and *CEO of Rebel Ink Publishing*, Ras Heru's creative and professional endeavors are manifests of his mission to build, rebuild, and establish progressive relationships between people and communities via art, culture, and literary craft. Ras Heru's first full-volume collection of poems, entitled *The Book of Heru: A Poet's* was published in 2018.

Made in the USA
Monee, IL
07 July 2026